Jeremiah A. Denton, Jr.
Vietnam War Hero

Anne Chancey Dalton

Seacoast Publishing
Birmingham, Alabama

Jeremiah A. Denton, Jr.: Vietnam War Hero

Published by Seacoast Publishing, Inc.
1149 Mountain Oaks Drive
Birmingham, Alabama 35226

Library of Congress Control Number: 2012930099

Cover art by Thomas B. Moore

ISBN 978-1-59421-078-5

To obtain copies of this book, please write or call:
Seacoast Publishing, Inc.
Post Office Box 26492
Birmingham, Alabama 35260
(205) 979-2909

Contents

About The Series

Alabama Roots is a book series designed to pro-vide reading pleasure for young people, to allow readers to better know the men and women who shaped the State of Alabama, and to fill a much-needed void of quality regional non-fiction for students in middle grades.

For years, teachers and librarians have searched for quality biographies about famous people from Alabama. This series is a response to that search. The series will cover a span of time from pre-statehood through the modern day.

The goal of *Alabama Roots* is to provide biogra-phies that are historically accurate and as interesting as the characters whose lives they explore.

The *Alabama Roots* mark assures readers and educators of consistent quality in research, composi-tion, and presentation.

It is a joint publishing project of Seacoast Publish-ing, Inc., and Will Publishing, Inc., both located in Birmingham, Alabama.

Dedication

This book is dedicated to the Denton children—all
extraordinary individuals: Jerry, Don, Jim, Bill,
Madeleine, Mike and Mary.

and

In memory of Jane Maury Denton—a woman of faith
and courage.
In honor of Admiral Jeremiah A. Denton—a hero
among us.

Writing This Book

The long journey has been exciting! I met people who not only provided information, but who also became friends.

Problems to solve included: writing stories about the life of a POW with suitable information for young people; meeting the needs of students studying the Vietnam Era; and my desire to be accurate.

I had watched the news coverage of Captain Jeremiah A. Denton, Jr. when he came off the plane on February 12, 1973, at Clark Air Base in the Philippines. I was deeply touched as he spoke for the first group of Prisoners of War coming back from North Vietnam. I told my husband, Perry, "Some day I want to write a book about him!"

I met Jane and Jerry Denton at an event in 2002 when Mobile celebrated its 300th birthday. Afterward, I talked with Jane and liked her immediately. She was friendly, calm and patient as she waited for Jerry.

I started this exciting journey by reading two books. *When Hell Was in Session* with Ed Brandt tells Jerry's story as a prisoner of war in North Vietnam. Joseph P. Duggan wrote *Jeremiah Denton: A Political Portrait,* which described Denton's years as a U.S. Senator for the State of Alabama.

Books by fellow POWs provided more details about Jerry's courageous leadership: *The Passing of the Night* by General Robinson Risner and *In Love and War* by Vice Admiral James and Sybil Stockdale.

I had two long interviews with Jerry—mostly covering his childhood. Then in 2010, we had a phone interview. Even with his busy schedule, he has been very helpful. His children have shared invaluable information and family stories.

Leo Denton, Jerry's youngest brother, has provided excellent information and help. He copied pictures and notes from his Baby Book. The notes written by his mother told about the boys' childhood. As Leo and I toured Mobile, he told stories about places important to his family.

My greatest resource when writing about Jane came from my own experiences. I helped raise five teenagers and two younger children—with the help of my husband and mother-in-law.

I did research at the University of South Alabama Archives; the Mobile Public Library—Local History and Genealogy Archives, including newspapers; the USS Alabama Battleship Memorial Park—the Denton Room and an A6 Intruder plane; the Museum of Mobile; and the National Naval Aviation Museum in Pensacola; McGill-Toolen High School—*McGillian* newspapers;

and Spring Hill College—*Springhillian* articles.

Thanks and appreciation to the following and those unintentionally omitted:

Claire Laird, Ellen Reilly, Sue Lyon, Marcelle Naman, Marion Watts, and Father Cunningham at St. Mary's Catholic Church and school; Judy Gibson, Sharon Peterson & Brother Paul Mulligan, SC at McGill-Toolen Catholic High School; Patricia Jones and Richard Weaver at Spring Hill College; Richard Bussel, El Paso County Historical Society; librarians at Chilton-Clanton Public Library; Jane's sister—Madeleine Maury McPhillips; Jane's close friend—Millie Cowan Hollinger, and Perilla Wilson, all from Mobile; Andy Sizemore—Birmingham Zoo; Chris Mitchell—Texas Parks & Wildlife Department; Scotty Kirkland–USA Photo Archives; Kevin and Shari Oakes—a super Navy family; Judy Marshall, Jane's hairstylist; internet friends: Bon, Sheila and Madeleine; the Leaky Pens; Montgomery writers; Carolyn Yoder—mentor and friend; and Kent Brown—Highlights Foundation.

Extra thanks to Doris-Jean Peak and Bon Latino who critiqued the manuscript; Dot Roper, my 91-year-old mother-in-law; and Jan and Tom Bailey—friends who publish books that influence lives.

Words can't express my love and appreciation for my husband, Perry, and our gigantic family.

Anne Chancey Dalton

Prologue

SUNDAY, JULY 18, 1965 dawned hot and cloud-less. The blue-green Gulf of Tonkin, part of the South China Sea west of the Philippines, stretched out below.

Jerry Denton, flight leader of Attack Squadron Seventy-five, led twenty-eight planes in a V-formation.

It was his twelfth combat flight. This time, the targets were warehouses filled with military equipment. Seventy-five miles south of Hanoi—capital city of North Vietnam—anti-aircraft guns protected the warehouses. Five U.S. planes had already been shot down while trying to attack the area.

It was a short flight from the aircraft carrier to the warehouses—about half an hour. Jerry soon saw the flat sandy coastline of North Vietnam. He glimpsed small green squares—flooded rice fields.

The planes began a rollercoaster ride toward the warehouses. Jerry radioed the other pilots: "Rainbow Flight from Rainbow Leader, target at ten o'clock. . . Rainbow Leader rolling in. . . ."

Jerry's crewman, twenty-two-year-old Lieutenant Bill Tschudy, sat slightly below Jerry to the right. Bill called out altitude every thousand feet as they roared swiftly toward the target.

Jerry lined up a large, square warehouse and pressed a button that released one of the eighteen, 500-pound bombs that he carried. "Suddenly, the plane felt as if its left wheel ran over a curb while taxiing," Jerry said later. "The radio whined loudly and went dead.

"I knew we'd been hit."

Jerry glanced at Bill who was taking pictures of the warehouse they had just bombed, unaware of their danger. Jerry couldn't tell him or other pilots. His radio and intercom systems had been destroyed.

The sky filled with black smoke from the North Vietnamese anti-aircraft guns. Jerry fought to get his plane under control. His seat jerked to the right, and the controls failed.

The plane rolled to the right. Jerry slammed his left foot hard on the rudder to keep the plane level. A sharp pain shot up his leg as a tendon snapped in his left thigh. It curled up into his lower abdomen. When it broke through the skin of his thigh, Jerry said it felt like someone had stabbed him. But he couldn't worry about that; too many other things were happening.

The plane slowly rolled into a level position. Jerry hit Bill on the shoulder, pointed upward and then made pulling gestures on the ejection bar. Then he yanked down on it and shot out of the plane. Bill quickly followed.

As his parachute floated downward, Jerry planned his escape. He hoped to land in or near the flooded rice fields. He and Bill would leave the parachutes and hide until dark. Then they'd wait to be picked up by a helicopter.

Jerry saw an American plane speeding in their direction. When the enemy anti-aircraft guns blasted away, it pulled up, circled and started back.

His buddies were coming to their rescue. But Jerry knew most of their planes carried only rockets and bombs. They had no guns for protective cover.

The wind blew Jerry and Bill back toward a bridge. Bill disappeared in the black smoke. Jerry's heart sank, but he stayed focused. *He would escape.*

As he looked down, Jerry knew his escape plan would fail.

Right below him, he saw about thirty North Vietnamese soldiers lining the banks of the swift Ma River. With guns pointed up at him, they waited for him to reach the ground.

Airplanes and Ships

THE NORTH VIETNAMESE SOLDIERS captured Jerry, and for the next seven years, he was their prisoner. At first, they kept him at a place that prisoners of war called the Hanoi Hilton. But it was not like any hotel that he'd ever seen.

Jerry had seen plenty of nice hotels. In fact, he didn't live in a house until he was almost seven. He lived in hotels with shiny marble floors. And huge glittering lights hanging from the ceilings. Orchestras played music in beautiful dining rooms.

Jeremiah A. Denton, Jr. was born in Mobile Maternity House July 15, 1924. His parents, Irene and Jeremiah, Sr., took him home to the Cawthon Hotel. That's where his grandfather, Peyton Steele, was manager. Jerry's father worked for him.

Being the first grandchild, Jerry took center stage for the next three years.

Jerry liked to go to a dining room on the hotel's rooftop. From there, he watched sailboats and ships on Mobile Bay.

The hotel was only a few blocks from the city docks. Jerry loved to go there with his father and grandfather. He watched tugboats pull huge ships into the Port of Mobile.

Jerry had toy boats, too. He played with them in the deep claw-

Young Jerry with his father.

foot tub in their hotel bathroom. "I loved playing with boats in the tub, just like all kids," he said.

At age two, Jerry, his family and grandparents moved to another hotel. This one was in El Paso, Texas, where Grandfather Steele had gone to manage the Sheldon Hotel. Jerry's father became his assistant. A handsome man who enjoyed talking with guests, Jerry's father made a good hotel manager. Soon, he became manager of the Fisher Hotel, also in El Paso.

Jerry's third birthday turned out to be a hint of things to come. He told hotel guests that he was having a party. Family and friends gathered in a private dining room decorated with colorful

Jerry Denton as a toddler dressed in a sailor suit.

balloons and streamers. Jerry blew out the candles on the cake and ripped into his presents.

The last present was the most special. Jerry's father pushed the final gift out of its hiding place and Jerry squealed and clapped his hands. It was a blue and gold airplane, and big enough to ride. His father helped Jerry into the airplane's seat, and he pedaled around the room. "For years, I dreamed that I could actually fly the plane," said Jerry later.

When he was grown up, Jerry got another plane. It made him even happier, because he could really fly it.

Rattlesnakes

EL PASO SITS on dry and mountainous ground
near where the Rio Grande River separates Texas from
Mexico.

Groves of pecan trees hugged the river. The trees
attracted many birds, including doves, that people
hunted with shotguns.

Jerry's father hunted the doves, and it became one
of his favorite sports. The idea of hunting excited six-
year-old Jerry too, and he asked his father if he could
go with him. His father liked that idea. He thought
Irene overprotected the boys. He wanted Jerry to
spend more time with him.

The first time Jerry went hunting, he just watched.
But back at the hotel, he bragged, "My Dad took me
hunting with his friends."

Soon, Jeremiah bought Jerry his own .410 shotgun. It weighed less than most shotguns. And when he
fired the gun, it didn't hurt as much when it slammed
against his shoulder. Dove hunting along the Rio

Grande began early. The doves roosted in or near the groves to sleep. About sunrise, they headed toward the river and on to their feeding grounds, then returning at sunset.

Hunters usually left El Paso before daylight. They chose a location with pecan groves to their backs and the Rio Grande River in front of them.

In the fall, Jerry begged to go hunting again. Now that Jeremiah managed the Fisher Hotel, he had problems getting away. But he could go Saturday afternoon. That way they'd be in place before sunset, ready when the doves returned.

His father's two friends met them at the hotel about the middle of the afternoon. They put all the guns on the floorboard and climbed into the back seat of the Model A Ford. Jerry sat beside his father on the front seat.

Once they were out of the city, Jerry gazed at the mountains on the left. Mountains in Mexico lay ahead on the right. Between them grew desert plants—spiny shrubs of mesquite, cactus, and tall yucca plants with stiff sword-sharp leaves.

Finally, Jerry saw groves of pecan trees. His father turned onto a rutted dirt road even bumpier than the one they'd been on. They passed a barn and drove to a field between the pecan grove and the river.

Talking and laughing, they climbed out of the car, got their guns and headed toward the field. Jerry's father kept looking at the sky. Lightening flashed in the distance.

The men settled into their positions, and it wasn't long before a flock of doves flew over. Jerry aimed his gun toward the sky, just like the men, and fired when they did. He scrambled to find the doves he'd shot.

Suddenly, Jerry smelled the scent of coming rain. He saw the heavy sheets of rain rolling toward them.

Everybody grabbed their guns and ran as rain and hail beat down. They were closer to the barn than the car so they dashed to it.

"My dad flung open the door, and we heard a loud, unearthly buzzing," said Jerry years later. "Standing in the doorway, we saw what looked like a hundred rattlesnakes. We froze for a second, watching them. Some slithered over the barn floor. But many rose up, shook their rattles, and hissed."

Hail or no hail, the hunters made a beeline for the car. Crying and stumbling, Jerry squeezed his father's hand in a viselike grip as they ran. The snakes terrified him and the hail hurt.

After the storm, the men went back hunting. But Jerry cried and didn't want to go. He feared seeing more snakes.

"Why are snakes in the barn?" he asked.

His father told Jerry that the nights were getting colder. The snakes needed to make a den, a place to sleep during the winter. Rats came into the barn to eat the farm animals' grain. And snakes ate the rats.

Jerry asked why the snakes raised up and shook their rattles and hissed. His father told him that's the way they scared off an enemy. If the enemy didn't leave, then the snake bit him.

He warned Jerry to watch out for snakes, since he might see one in the field. But he didn't need to fear seeing a lot of them like in the barn.

Jerry wasn't convinced and still wanted to stay in the car. His father asked if he'd had fun hunting. When Jerry nodded, his father opened the car door and told him to get out. They went back hunting.

Moving

BY THE TIME the Dentons moved back to Mobile in 1931, the year Jerry turned seven, America was in the middle of the Great Depression. Many people were out of work. Few had any money.

There were new things in the Denton family, though. Jerry had a little brother, Peyton, who was nearly four, and before the year was over he had

Home on Mobile's Hallett Street where Jerry lived when he was seven.

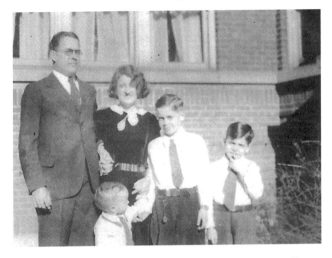

The Denton family: Jeremiah, Irene, Jerry, Peyton (far right) and Leo at apartment in Chicago.

another baby brother, Leo. The family had a new experience—living in a house instead of a hotel. His father rented a house on South Hallett Street, only a mile west of downtown Mobile. The street had a couple of huge old homes with tall white columns and large lawns. However, several young couples with children lived in new one-story houses.

Jeremiah no longer managed a hotel. He had taken a job as a traveling salesman and was out of town a lot. In fact, he was out of town so much that they moved from Mobile to Chicago where they would be close to Irene's grandmother, aunts and uncle.

The Dentons moved into an apartment on a shady street with a big park across the street, where Jerry and his brothers could play. To Jerry, it was a wonderful place.

His father, Jeremiah, brought home a puppy that they named Skippy. Jerry couldn't have been happier than when playing with his new pet.

On weekends the family went out to the Edgewater Beach Hotel, where several members of Irene's well-to-do family lived. It sat right on the shore of Lake Michigan and there was a beach for swimming.

Irene dressed up the boys in Buster Brown outfits—smock-like tops with big white collars, bloomer pants and stockings above their knees. That wasn't the favorite thing for Jerry and his brothers, but they had lived in hotels so often that they were used to dressing up. More fun to them was listening to big bands and famous musicians play at the hotel. Once a band director even handed Jerry his baton and let him lead the band!

As fun as it was for Jerry, it was much less so for his father, Jeremiah.

Irene's wealthy relatives bought expensive gifts and clothes for the boys, and it bothered Jeremiah that he didn't have enough money to buy them himself. He was embarrassed not to have the money.

"Dad read about the trouble in Europe," said Jerry. "He believed the United States would soon get involved in a World War. If that happened, he predicted

Houston would become a boom town. He wanted to get a job there. But my mother didn't want to move. She thought a boom town would ruin our family life."

Jeremiah kept looking for a better job, and thinking that Houston was the place to go. But Irene never was convinced.

Then, when Jeremiah came home one day to find the apartment filled with new furniture, the family broke apart. Jeremiah had not bought the furniture. His wealthy in-laws had bought it.

"When he discovered Mother's relatives had bought it, that was the final blow to his pride.

"Dad was furious," said Jerry years later. "My parents got into big arguments, when my mother refused to move. Finally, my parents separated. Dad left for Houston alone."

The boys missed their father—as did Irene.

They all hoped he would come home.

But he didn't come home and by the Christmas holidays of 1935, Irene no longer had enough money to keep the family in Chicago.

She moved back to Mobile where her father was then managing the Bienville Hotel.

He said they could live at the hotel until they could get a place of their own.

The Bienville Hotel was decked out in holiday

trimmings when Irene and the boys arrived. An orchestra played Christmas music in the glittering dining rooms.

Grandfather and Grandmother Steele welcomed the boys and Irene with open arms. Once again, they shared a suite of rooms. They spent time with Jerry and his brothers and gave them gifts.

But it didn't make up for their father not being there.

Jerry's mother went to work, first at the Bienville, and later at the nearby Battle House, Mobile's largest hotel, where she stayed for many years as the manager's secretary.

The boys enrolled at St. Mary's Catholic School where Jerry had finished second grade. He was now in sixth, Peyton in third, and Leo started his first day of kindergarten. "I missed my friends in Chicago," said Jerry, "but I got involved in sports as well as school and church activities."

After several years, Irene's parents helped her buy a house less than two miles west of the Bienville Hotel. "When we moved into the house on Providence Street, I really felt settled for the first time," said Jerry.

"St. Mary's Convent and the school playground sat directly across the street," said Leo. "The school went through eighth grade. So, the older kids played basket-ball and touch football on the playground in the after-noons."

"I grew up hearing the 'Bells of St. Mary's' mark the hour until 9 p.m. Chimes played hymns several times a day," said Jerry. "The church surrounded our lives and activities."

The Denton family enjoyed making music when the boys were older. Irene was an excellent pianist. Jerry played the trumpet; Peyton the saxophone; and Leo the clarinet. The little band performed at family gatherings. They also entertained the nuns and priests when they came over. And Jerry sometimes sang solos at church.

"The stay in Mobile turned out to be one of the happiest periods of my life," said Jerry. "We saw our father from time to time, but it wasn't the same. A couple of years later, he moved back to Mobile for awhile. In Texas, he worked at a shipyard. Later, he went into the real estate business."

But he never lived with Irene and the boys as a family again.

Close Calls

"REGARDLESS OF WHERE WE LIVED, I was teased about my accent—Southern, Texan or Yankee," said Jerry. "One boy constantly bullied me. He got right in my face, sneered and said, 'You talk like this...' and mimicked me. So I tried to copy his accent so he wouldn't beat me up again. But it didn't work!"

Jerry's father got tired of hearing about the bullies. He told Jerry that a bully wouldn't be a bully unless he was a coward.

A professional boxer named Tommy Littleton had trained Jeremiah to box in Mobile. And Jeremiah continued boxing in the Navy. So he taught Jerry self-defense when they lived in Chicago. It worked, but it sometimes got Jerry into trouble, especially as he got older.

When Jerry was in his early teens, neighborhood kids hung out at Lyons Park. They swam, played tennis and other sports and, sometimes, just hung around and goofed off.

One day at the park, Jerry was talking to a girl that he liked.

Another boy liked the girl too. When he saw Jerry talking with her, he came up and began making smart remarks to provoke a fight. "Since Dad had taught me to box, I figured I was a much better fighter," Jerry recalled. "A few well placed punches can really hurt a person. So to avoid that, I turned and walked away. But he followed yelling threats!

"I worked at a Gulf Service Station a block away. Mr. Black, the owner, didn't allow fights on his property. So I headed toward the station, hoping to get there before it closed. (It just so happened that on that day) the city softball playoffs were at the McGill baseball field across from the station. I dodged in and out of the crowd going to the game. When I got within sight of the station, I saw it was closed. The bully was gaining on me, so I hurried across the street. The crowd was thicker near the entrance gate, and I hoped to lose him. But he caught me.

"I told him I didn't want to fight. But he took a couple of swings at me anyway. I hit him early on the jaw and broke my right thumb. Since I couldn't use it, I...hit him with my left. People going to the game stared at us. By the time some men pulled us apart, the guy was in bad shape.

"Fortunately, a University Military School football player saw the whole thing. He said, 'Jerry didn't start the fight.' Then he told them exactly what happened. (The football player) speaking up in my defense meant a lot to me."

Jerry found himself in another sticky mess while growing up in Mobile, and this one had nothing to do with bullies.

It was a day when he and a friend made foolish mistakes and except for pure luck, Jerry could have killed himself.

He and his friends often fished and hunted birds on Mobile Bay—sometimes hunting and fishing on the same trip.

"(We) carried our guns in the rowboat in case we spotted a flock of birds," said Jerry.

On one particular trip, the boys were

Jerry, standing foreground, and his brother, Peyton, in back, on one of many Mobile Bay fishing trips.

"catching fish right and left." They lost track of time and the tide—which was pulling water out of the bay. "When we started back, the boat got stuck about half-a-mile from shore. We climbed out and sank knee-deep in mud. We struggled, pushing the boat foot-by-foot toward shore. Suddenly, a flock of pink birds landed nearby. So we grabbed our guns out of the boat.

"A woman standing on shore watched us. Seeing the guns, she waved her arms. 'Hey, boys!' she yelled. 'Don't you know what those are? They are flamingoes! Don't shoot them!'"

"We put the guns away—until she left.

"Then I reached into the boat and got my .410 double-barreled shotgun. It had to be cocked. Stuck in the mud, I couldn't climb into the boat to do it. I tried several times, but it wouldn't cock. So, I stuck the barrel in my stomach to keep it out of the mud. I pulled again as hard as I could, and I heard the gun go 'click.' But it didn't fire. I guess it had gotten wet. And that saved my life!"

Skipping School

TARZAN BOOKS and black and white movies inspired adventure. In Jerry's early teens, neighborhood boys made their own jungle quests in the swampy land around Mobile. Near St. Mary's School, drainage-ditch water flowed into a large cement culvert. Two blocks later, it surfaced as a little creek and made its way through a swamp.

"The culvert looked like a long dark tunnel," said Jerry. "We ducked our heads and stumbled through as spider webs brushed our faces. Bugs crawled on our necks and arms. And fear of snakes kept us alert!

"We'd burst out of the dark tunnel into our own amazing jungle," said Jerry. Spanish moss dangled from huge old oak trees. The boys used thick vines to swing like Tarzan. Whoopin', hollerin' and acting tough, they explored for hours.

Most students at St. Mary's School lived in the neighborhood. During lunch break, they either went home to eat or brought a lunch to school. One spring day when Jerry was in eighth grade, a group of boys sat at a picnic table on the playground, eating their sandwiches and, as usual, complaining about school.

"Let's take off and go to the creek," said Jerry.

"At first, they thought I was teasing and just laughed," he said later. "But, I said, 'If we leave right now, we can have some fun.'"

Some girls overheard the conversation and asked if they could go too. "Before we got a block away, the rest of our class caught up with us—about twenty-five in all.

"The girls giggled and acted silly all the way through the tunnel," said Jerry. "But when I led them out into the warm sunshine in the jungle, they stood

This culvert was the tunnel leading to the "amazing jungle."

silently in awe.

"Caught up exploring, we forgot the time. A girl panicked when she realized lunch break had been over an hour. I said, 'School lets out in another hour. And we're already in as much trouble as we can get in. Why not enjoy the rest of the afternoon? Then we go straight home. The whole class won't be expelled. If no one tells whose idea it was, everything will be okay.'

"But it wasn't fun after that. Everybody, especially the girls, worried about what would happen if the school contacted our parents. I knew that wasn't likely. Most of the students didn't have telephones in their homes. Surely Sister Mary Josephine wouldn't go to everybody's house that night.

"As I expected, Sister Mary Josephine and Father O'Donoghue waited until the next morning to deal with the problem," said Jerry. "All the eighth graders were called into the auditorium. It didn't take long to determine that the girls weren't involved in the planning. So they were dismissed. Then they questioned the boys. Finally, it was down to just three. After lengthy questioning, I admitted it was my idea.

"Sister Mary Josephine talked to me about an hour," said Jerry. "She said, 'It takes leadership to do what you've done. If you have that much influence over people, you had better be very careful how you use it!'"

Years later in a faraway land Jerry had to make a decision, and he remembered Sister Mary Josephine's words. On that day in North Vietnam's Hanoi Hilton prison, Jerry knew that if he stepped forward and took leadership, he would be tortured. If he kept quiet, he'd stay out of a whole lot of trouble.

He remembered Sister Mary Josephine, and he stepped forward.

But a lot of things would happen in Jerry's life before that day came.

High School

McGILL INSTITUTE, a Catholic high school for boys in Mobile, had more than 300 students.

The school stood a few blocks west of the Government Street waterfront, blending in with the beautiful old mansions that lined the street.

Jerry did not blend in. Among the 300 students, he stood out as a popular leader, an athlete, a scholar.

An article about Jerry appeared in the school newspaper, the *McGillian*. Entitled *Jerry Denton— Senior of the Month—Active Athlete, Class President*, the article listed things about him. Favorite things: hobbies—girls and memorizing poetry. Sports—football. Subject—English. School activities: drama and glee clubs (often with leading roles and solos), newspaper staff and Confraternity (a Catholic youth group that stressed spiritual growth). He also made the honor roll and won popularity contests: "Biggest Socialite" (invited to many parties), "Ideal McGillian," and "Most Popular."

Mobile's historic McGill Institute on Government Street where Jerry went to high school. (Used with permission)

Playing sports taught Jerry lessons that stuck with him throughout his life. In addition to football, he pitched on the baseball team, and played forward on the basketball team. He also played golf and tennis—winning an intramural tennis championship.

The McGill Yellow Jackets tried for the City Championship during Jerry's senior year. "I played my best as quarterback, but we lost. Totally exhausted, I had a bleeding face and a tooth knocked out," said Jerry. "But Coach Overton surprised me. He told the team, 'Denton rose to the occasion. He has that in him. If all of you had played like he did, we would have won.'"

The 1941 football team; Jerry is number 20 on the second row.

Jerry wrote editorials (articles giving his opinions) for the *McGillian*. One involved students' dreams, goals and choices made during high school. He listed questions each student should ask. *What are my dreams for my life? How can I reach my goals? Who and what am I going to follow?* Jerry believed answers to these questions helped determine a student's life.

Jerry's life has shown this to be true. "I made up my mind about my future in the tenth grade," he said. "I saw the movie—*Navy, Blue and Gold*—about the Naval Academy. Since things came easy for me, I loafed along. However, at Annapolis, I'd have to do my best to survive. I believed I could give my all to being a naval officer. So I set a goal—attend the Naval Academy."

A student couldn't just apply to the Naval Academy like to a college. His congressman had to back him. So, Brother Gerald, principal of McGill, wrote to Congressman Frank Boykin. He told why he thought Jerry made a good candidate for the Naval Academy. Later, Jerry learned that seventy-one other Alabama students also wanted to attend.

As he neared the end of his senior year, Jerry heard nothing about an appointment to the Naval Academy. He could only wait and wonder.

In December, five months before the end of Jerry's senior year, something happened that changed his life, and the life of every United States citizen.

On December 7, 1941, the Japanese attacked American ships and military installations in Hawaii, at a place called Pearl Harbor.

The next day America declared war on Japan.

Soon after, America also was at war with Germany and Italy.

Many men and women joined the military to fight. Others went to work in factories to build planes and ships and weapons to fight with.

Even when he graduated from McGill Institute five months later, Jerry still had heard nothing about an appointment to the Naval Academy, although he still wanted to go there.

Instead of sitting around and waiting, he signed up for summer classes at Spring Hill College in Mobile.

And he fell in love.

A young and attractive Jane Maury, who would win Jerry's heart when she was older.

Jane

THE MAJOR EVENT of Jerry's summer after graduation occurred on a Saturday hayride. He took a date, but another fellow's date caught his eye. Her name was Jane Maury, a beautiful sixteen-year-old with shiny brown hair and sparkling brown eyes. She had just finished tenth grade at the Convent of Visitation, a high school for girls.

From Jane's quiet conversation, it was evident that she was intelligent, and her charming personality captivated Jerry. She laughed easily without being silly. And she showed sincere interest in other people—what they thought and had to say. She also expressed her own ideas.

As Jane and Jerry talked, they realized they were both members of St. Mary's Church. No doubt they had seen each other. But the large church held Mass at various times. Jerry was a couple of years older, so they weren't involved in the same activities.

Before the day was over, Jane had captured Jerry's

heart, even though she wasn't his date for that evening.

He decided right then that one day Jane Maury would be his bride. Wisely, he did not tell her until much later.

Jane went home and told her younger sister, Madeleine, all about the hayride. She said that she met the most handsome boy with beautiful white teeth.

The next morning, Jane and her family went to St. Mary's Church as usual. When they entered the sanctuary, Jerry was an usher. Jane had already told her family about him. So she whispered to her mother and pointed to him.

She was as smitten with Jerry as Jerry was with her.

Anne Chancey Dalton

College and Naval Academy

SPRING HILL COLLEGE'S 1942 summer session
was over and Jerry still had no word about the Naval
Academy appointment. So he signed up for the next
semester at Spring Hill.

He was a popular student, and was elected president of the freshman class.

Jerry had joined the Naval Reserve shortly after
the bombing of Pearl Harbor. The summer of 1943
rolled around and Jerry still had no word from the
Naval Academy. So during that summer, he went to
boot camp at a reserve midshipmen's school in Mississippi. There he studied math and science and faced
hard physical training. Through that program, named
the V-12 College Training Program, he worked toward
a college degree at Spring Hill and a commission in
the Navy at the same time.

One day the commanding officer at the school called Jerry to his office. When Jerry walked in, the commanding officer boomed, "Denton! Denton! You're going to Bancroft Hall!"

Jerry in his Naval Reserve uniform.

Jerry just stared at him. He had no idea what that meant. However, he quickly learned he had gotten the appointment to Annapolis!

A few months later, he found himself living in Bancroft Hall with the academy's other midshipmen.

Jerry and Jane dated while he was at the Naval Academy.

She graduated first in her high

school class then enrolled at Mary Washington College in Virginia, only ninety miles from Jerry.

At the Naval Academy chapel, Jerry sang in the choir. He also learned about moral courage in military leadership.

His time in Annapolis passed quickly. World War II ended with an American victory. A year later, on June 5, 1946, Jerry graduated with honors and became an officer—an Ensign—in the United States Navy.

Jane's family drove from Mobile to Annapolis for June Week. It included military ceremonies, parties and dances before graduation.

The next day, June 6, 1946, Jane and Jerry married at the Naval Academy Chapel. Mobile friends served as bridesmaids with Jane's sister, Madeleine, the maid of honor.

Six midshipmen served as ushers. After seating the last guests, they hooked on their swords and wore them until time for a special ceremony. It was called the arch of swords ceremony. As the bride and groom left the chapel, the ushers formed an arch with their swords. The newlywed couple walked down the steps and passed under the arch of swords. It was an old custom that represented a promise to the newly married couple. Their Navy family promised to give them

Happy newlyweds—Jerry and Jane on their wedding day.

help and support whenever needed.

At that happy moment, neither Jerry nor Jane had any idea just how much help and support they would need in years to come.

Navy Family

TIME AND PLACES seemed to fly by for the Jerry Denton family.

Sometimes literally.

Jerry earned the wings of a Naval aviator.

Ships and airplanes took him to many different places.

He trained to fight naval battles, tested airplanes, taught others to fly and led groups of pilots as a squadron commander.

And Jerry and Jane added sons to their family— Jerry, Don, Jim and Bill.

Jerry had jobs in the Mediterranean, and the family lived in France, where daughter, Madeleine, was born.

He learned to take off from and land on an aircraft carrier.

By 1960, there were six Denton children ages 1 to 13, including Michael.

As the children got older, they were involved in

The Denton children in a Christmastime photo while their father was a POW. Back row, from left, are Bill, Madeleine and Jerry. Front row, from left, are Mary, Don, Mike and Jim.

sports. When Jerry's schedule allowed, he took an active part. Middle-school-age son, Don, thought those years were some of his best times with his father. One year, Jerry was assistant coach to an all-white Junior League football team. A black boy tried out, and Jerry accepted him on the team. However, some league organizers strongly objected. They claimed an unwritten rule didn't allow blacks players in the league. At this time, people across the nation were standing up for racial justice. And that is what Jerry did. He fought all the way to city hall for the boy's rights. The black boy became a member of the team. At the end of the season, his white teammates elected him Sportsman of the Year.

In 1963, the Denton family lived in Newport, Rhode Island. Daughter, Mary Elizabeth, the seventh Denton child was born, bringing the total to five boys and two girls.

"This was a happy time for our family," said Don. "Dad was at home, not leaving for long tours of sea duty. On weekends that fall, the four older sons played touch football with Dad. During our only New England winter, we often sledded down a long steep hill. Sometimes, we played handball at the War College gym. Spring brought tennis and sailing. The family also enjoyed outings in our powder blue Plymouth Fury convertible. We loved that car."

The family had fun, but Jerry was strong-willed and strict. He expected the children to live up to his standards, both in how they lived and how they treated other people.

"At age fifteen, I was well aware of black people struggling for equal rights," said Don. "We watched the violence used against them to stop protests and demonstrations. Above all, I remember the March on Washington in August. Our family felt something important was happening. We watched it with Mom and Dad on our black and white TV. Dr. Martin Luther King's 'I Have a Dream' speech stirred us. Of course, our parents helped us understand all of this. They had been mostly raised in the Deep South. But overall, they approved of racial integration and the Blacks' struggle for freedom.

"John Kennedy was President," said Don. "We saw him once in Newport, entering a church with daughter Caroline. Our family identified with the big Kennedy extended family. And both our families were Catholic. We also watched them on TV play touch football on the White House lawn. This was just weeks before the assassination."

On November 22, 1963, President John F. Kennedy was shot and killed. Only seven years older than Jerry, the Navy war hero was a role model. The day of his assassination was the first time the Denton children saw their father cry.

Capture

BY THE 1960s, Jerry had earned the rank of commander and was flying fighter jets off the aircraft carrier *Independence*. The family lived in Virginia Beach, Virginia, near the carrier's port of Norfolk.

It was 1965. America was deep in the Vietnam War, and the *Independence* was ordered to go to the Gulf of Tonkin. Part of the South China Sea, the Gulf washed ashore on the eastern coast of North Vietnam.

Jerry was going to war.

Jane and the children understood Jerry being away from home. It happened often with Navy families. However, this assignment involved real danger, something that Jerry was about to face for the first time after twenty years in the Navy.

When Jerry told the family goodbye, Jane said, "I hope you'll be home by Christmas!"

Jerry wanted that too, but he didn't want to get Jane's hopes too high. "The war will last a long time," he said.

Jerry as a combat pilot during the Vietnam War.

A couple of months later, with Jerry off on the other side of the world, Jane hustled the younger kids into the car. "The M Society"—Madeleine, Michael and Mary Beth—wanted to see *Mary Poppins* at the drive-in theater.

To Jane's surprise, in the middle of the movie, tears streamed down her face. She didn't worry about Jerry—he was an experienced pilot. So, why this sudden feeling that he faced great danger? With the twelve-hour time difference, Sunday morning had already arrived on his ship. Jerry probably planned to enjoy a day off. But still, she cried silently.

On July 18, 1965, Jerry felt tense—like before one

of his big football games in high school.

The United States was fiercely bombing North Vietnam targets. The Navy called the series of bombing raids "Rolling Thunder."

On this day, Jerry would lead his men on a dangerous "Rolling Thunder" raid.

As Jerry worked through the check list before taking off from the *Independence*, his tenseness faded and his self-confidence returned. At age forty-one, he was in good shape physically and mentally. He had already flown eleven combat missions; he felt experienced. In just two days, Commander Jeremiah Denton would become commanding officer of Attack Squadron Seventy-five.

Secretary of Defense Robert S. McNamara was the man that U.S. President Lyndon Johnson had chosen to be in charge of military forces.

On this day, McNamara had just arrived on the *Independence*. He had toured Vietnam to see what was going on. Since Jerry's squadron was the only one going on a mission that day, he came to watch it take off.

Dressed in civilian clothes, McNamara looked out of place on the flight deck. The coat of his expensive suit flapped in the strong wind. He wore huge earphones to quiet the roar of the jet engines. The earphones made him look like Mickey Mouse.

Still, funny as he looked, it was an honor to have him on board. To show respect, Denton saluted him through the plane's Plexiglas canopy as the plane taxied for take-off.

It seemed not important—the Secretary of Defense watching the squadron take off. At that moment there was no way Jerry could know how much suffering McNamara's being on deck that day would add to Jerry's life.

About forty-five minutes after lifting off the *Independence* deck, Jerry's life turned upside down. He saluted McNamara, flew to the target area, got hit by anti-aircraft guns, and ejected from his plane. Now, his parachute floated down toward armed North Vietnamese soldiers.

He released the parachute as he hit the cool, muddy water and swam underwater toward the middle of the river. A strong swimmer, Jerry realized he couldn't move his left leg. His heavy flight boots pulled him down.

He swallowed water and began choking. He had to surface or drown. He inflated one side of his life vest, and his head soon came out of the water.

North Vietnamese soldiers, 20 yards away on the

south riverbank, gestured for him to come ashore. Instead Jerry swam toward his survival gear. A soldier fired his rifle, and a bullet whizzed over Jerry's head.

Two young North Vietnamese men wearing loincloths put a bark canoe in the river from the north shore and paddled toward Jerry. He knew they wanted to capture him before the soldiers—hoping to get a reward.

A scar-faced young man in the front of the canoe wildly waved a machete over his head. The other man paddled.

Jerry reached his survival gear and inflated the one-man life raft. He threw the gear in and clung to the side. He couldn't climb in because of his injured leg.

The soldiers yelled at the men in the canoe, but they continued after Jerry. He also yelled and shoved the canoe back when it bumped him.

As the man in the front of the canoe swung the machete, Jerry turned away. The flat side of the blade hit him on the back. Twice the man cut Jerry deeply on the neck. Finally, he saw Jerry's injured leg and motioned to his partner for help.

The small men struggled to haul Jerry—5-foot-11 and 165 pounds—into the raft. He was dazed and bleeding. They tied his arms behind him and towed the raft to shore.

Soldiers pulled Jerry from the raft and pointed toward a path up a steep bank. He tried to walk, but his leg collapsed and he fell. The soldiers dragged him up the bank. Pain shot through Jerry's body, but he was so furious that he noticed neither pain or fear. Jerry couldn't believe he'd been shot down and captured!

Searching for weapons, the soldiers cut off Jerry's clothes down to his underwear.

Now, all his protection disappeared. They had his survival gear, someone took his watch, and he'd lost his gun when he ejected.

A soldier saw the tendon had come through the skin in his left thigh. Since Jerry couldn't walk, they put him on a plank. They raised it to their shoulders to carry him.

About that time, a U.S. Navy jet flew over the treetops. The soldiers dropped the plank and dove for cover. Jerry hit the ground and was knocked unconscious.

Jerry regained consciousness in time to see a plane again. It made two more low passes in spite of enemy guns firing at it. Then the jet circled away toward the south. His friends could not rescue him.

He was alone.

Captured.

Injured.

And unable to escape.

Prisoner of War

SOLDIERS CARRIED JERRY to a mud hut in a nearby village. Farmers with rakes and hoes and women with babies watched. Hurt and groggy, Jerry stared with surprise at their caring expressions. One patted him on the stomach. The soldiers lowered him to the dirt floor in the hut. His injured leg felt numb, but his lower stomach burned like fire. In a few minutes, a villager brought him a cup of tea and later warm coconut milk. The drinks helped revived him.

After a couple of hours, Jerry was taken by boat to another village. Soldiers took him off the boat to a waiting motorcycle with a sidecar. A soldier lowered him into the sidecar with his hurt leg hanging over the side. At the next village, the driver stopped the motorcycle amid a cloud of dust. To Jerry's surprise, his navigator, Bill Tschudy, who had bailed out at the same time as Jerry, walked through the dust toward him. Bill only had a moment to ask if Jerry was hurt before a soldier led him away.

The North Vietnamese displayed Jerry at a meeting hall in the village. Curious villagers crowded in to stare. Most North Vietnamese had never seen an American pilot. They saw cartoons of President Johnson and Secretary of Defense McNamara on posters or drawn on walls. They heard planes overhead and bombs exploding, but they had not seen *the enemy*.

When the villagers realized Jerry was badly hurt, most faces were kind. However, a young soldier motioned for Jerry to bow to him. Jerry refused. Angry and embarrassed, the soldier drew his gun and pressed the barrel to Jerry's head. The people gasped and backed away. Jerry lost consciousness.

The next thing he knew, Jerry was lying on a bamboo mat in a corner of the meeting hall. Two soldiers guarding him listened to a small radio near the door.

That evening, a nicely-dressed young woman gave Jerry two shots. He asked what they were in his limited French. She told him water and quinine to prevent malaria carried by mosquitoes.

An old man guarded Jerry through an agonizing night. The old man brought tea to him several times. About dark the next day, a truck came to pick him up. However, he was too weak to walk and passed out.

Jerry woke up in the back of a jeep. A blindfold covered his eyes, and his hands and feet were tied. Later, Jerry learned he was on his way to Hanoi with guards. The jeep stopped at a ferry landing. Jerry heard Bill's voice coming from a nearby jeep, loudly demanding water. Seven years would pass before Jerry again had direct contact with Bill.

The hot sun beat down in Hanoi that July morning when Jerry arrived. Sneaking a look from under his blindfold, he saw people walking down a wide tree-shaded boulevard. Lines of bicycles, military vehicles, trucks and a few cars moved along noisily. Hanoi, once capital of French Indochina, had become capital of North Vietnam. Just as French influence was evident in buildings and parks back home in Mobile, it was here also.

When the jeep stopped, Jerry again stole a quick glance from under his blindfold. He saw a steel gate built into a massive wall. The top—studded with large pieces of sharp glass—had barbed wire.

Workers waiting to go into the prison through a smaller gate stared at him. Newspapers, posters and cartoons showed horrible things Americans supposedly did to North Vietnamese. This made the people hate Americans and want to fight harder. A scowling, middle-aged woman charged Jerry and hit him in the face with her purse.

The jeep finally pulled through the main gate of Hoa Lo Prison. American prisoners of war (POWs) called it the Hanoi Hilton. The French-built prison covered a city block near the center of Hanoi. Red tile roofs sat atop the beige, stucco-walled buildings.

The jeep drove between two buildings and into a large courtyard. As Jerry learned later, the POWs had named many sections of the prison. To the left of the gate was New Guy Village containing only four cells. To the right was Las Vegas—the largest section with names of hotels like Stardust and the Golden Nugget. The jeep stopped in Heartbreak Courtyard with Heartbreak Hotel at the far end.

As a guard led Jerry between buildings, he heard a familiar sound. "I heard a low, rather mournful whistling. I strained my ears and glanced around. I couldn't find the source. However, the melody— *Yankee Doodle*—was unmistakable. My heart skipped a beat. I was not alone!"

Early Sunday morning in Virginia Beach, Jane got up thinking about her tears the night before. She wrote Jerry a letter, then got the family ready for church.

That afternoon, unexpected visitors came to the house. Twelve-year-old Bill called up the stairs, "Mom,

Captain Nelson is here to see you!"

The words fell on Jane like a load of bricks. Captain Nelson had gone to her neighbor's house a few days earlier. He told Bobi Boecker that her husband, Don, had been shot down over Laos. Now Captain Nelson stood in *their* house.

"It's all right—it's all right!" Captain Nelson called up the stairs. "We're trying to get Jerry out! You know we rescued Don!"

Jane came down the stairs silently. Mrs. Nelson, standing beside her husband, hugged Jane and said kind words. Then she led Jane to a couch in the living room. The usually no-nonsense Nelson hesitated and cleared his throat. "Jerry and Bill's parachutes were sighted, and guys from his squadron flew cover." He quickly added, "Don't worry. He landed in a river and made it safely to shore. A rescue effort is under way."

Jane didn't know what to do or say. Finally, she asked Billy to take Mary Beth, his eighteen-month-old sister, to Mrs. Armstrong's house across the street. Mrs. Nelson had seen Michael and Madeleine, ages six and eight, playing in the yard. She volunteered to take them as well. She'd let the Armstrongs, another Navy family, know the situation. Captain Nelson assured Jane that he would keep her informed. He told her to call them if they could do anything to help.

"Mr. Armstrong took Michael and me and his kids to the bike store," said Madeleine years later. "The news came on the car radio, and the announcer mentioned the first local pilots to be shot down. Mr. Armstrong quickly turned it off. Even as an eight-year-old, I recognized his kindness."

Jerry—the oldest Denton son—had graduated from high school about a month earlier. He pulled into the driveway, just returning from his first road trip in his dad's new convertible. He knew his mom had been concerned about him. However, he was surprised when she met him at the front door.

"My mother, with an unusual sense of calm, took me into the living room. We sat down, and she looked me in the eyes. 'Dad has been shot down,' she said with a slight catch in her voice. 'He's missing—but they saw a parachute.' I stared at my mother who looked and acted so young. None of us seven children were particularly well-behaved. Dad disciplined us, and now he was far away. I thought *I don't know how my mother is going to make it,*" said Jerry later.

Jane told Jerry the younger children were at the Armstrong's house. She wanted him to make sure his other three brothers didn't get into trouble while she was gone for awhile. Assured that her children were taken care of, Jane went to church and prayed.

When she came home, Jane got the younger children from the neighbor's house. Then, she did a quite ordinary thing. She checked to see if a rosebush she'd grown from a cutting needed water. Jane discovered it had bloomed.

"The first rose bloomed on the very day we learned that Dad had been shot down," said Madeleine. "Mom believed it was a message from God—that even when a situation seems impossible, there is always hope."

Shock

THE DENTON FAMILY tried to deal with the shock of learning that Jerry had been shot down. The children—frightened about their father—felt helpless. They watched their mother suffer anxiety and grief.

News of Jerry's capture spread quickly. Friends offered help and comfort. Jane's close friend in Washington came at once. Jane's sister, Madeleine, arrived from Mobile in a couple of days. She stayed several weeks and then took the youngest child, Mary Beth, home with her. Other family members kept in close contact and visited whenever possible.

After bringing the shocking news on Sunday afternoon, Captain Nelson came by Monday night. He showed Jane the spot on a map where Jerry was captured.

She already knew in her heart that Jerry wasn't going to be picked up. So she wasn't surprised when Captain Nelson said, "They called off the search."

To make matters worse, pictures of Jerry appeared

Friday on the noon news. Jane and Madeleine ate lunch at a friend's house and celebrated Madeleine's birthday. The TV was on. The women turned toward it when the newscaster announced two local men had been captured in Vietnam. They watched as photos showed Jerry and Bill Tschudy in their military uniforms.

Then another picture flashed on the screen, and Jane gasped. "Is that Jerry?" she screamed.

His face, swollen and out of shape, made it hard for Jane to recognize her husband of nineteen years. A Hanoi official stated that Denton and Tschudy had been sent by McNamara personally. Therefore, they would be treated as *war criminals*—not prisoners of war.

Jane broke down and cried. Jerry looked far worse than she had imagined.

How could he survive?

How could her family watch news broadcasts when one night it may show Jerry?

But how could they *not* watch and miss seeing him?

The First TV War

THE TUNE *YANKEE DOODLE* gave Jerry unexpected hope. Lieutenant John McKamey whistled the tune. He peeped through a hole in his cell door. Then he whistled to new arrivals as they were lead to New Guy Village.

Jerry's new home, Cell 4, measured nine by eight feet—the size of a bathroom at home. Two concrete beds filled most of the space. Stocks made from a wooden frame were attached to the beds. Each had two ankle spaces. A hinged metal part clamped down and locked the prisoner to the bed. A small pail used as a toilet sat in one corner. The door had a peephole that guards opened from the hall. From a barred window at the other end, Jerry could see the huge wall surrounding the prison.

Two soldiers came into Jerry's cell that afternoon and woke him from a deep sleep. "Get up," one said in English. "You are to be questioned."

"I scowled and pointed to my left thigh. I can't

walk!" said Jerry. "However, with the prodding of a bayonet, I crawled to a quiz room in another part of the prison. A guard roughly helped me up on a stool. Two self-important looking North Vietnamese men sat behind a table."

Prisoners of War called the plump scholarly-looking man in civilian clothes *Owl*. He'd once been a college professor. The other man, about thirty-years-old, wore an army uniform. Nicknamed *Eagle*, he claimed to be a combat pilot.

Jerry learned how to behave as a prisoner of war in Survival School. Even though weak and in horrible pain, he'd do his best to follow the American Fighting Man's Code of Conduct. *I will never surrender of my own free will. I will resist in every way possible.*

"To hide my fear, I tried to look calm but also show pride," said Jerry. "I wanted the courage to die rather than give them military information. I also didn't want to give them anything they could use against me. They had me, but they weren't going to enjoy it!"

Jerry, the first pilot of a fighter plane known as the A6 Intruder captured by the North Vietnamese, expected to be tortured for information about the new aircraft. However, he wasn't. "Early on, the North Vietnamese didn't torture anyone to my knowledge for military information," said Jerry. "When they tortured for that, they had pilots with more up-to-date information."

The Code of Conduct also stated: *When questioned...I am bound to give only name, rank, service number, and date of birth.* (The Big Four.) So Jerry gave that information.

Owl asked, 'What kind of plane were you flying?' Jerry refused to answer. The Code said: *I will evade answering further questions to the utmost of my ability.* Owl asked over and over and louder and louder. Furious, he finally sent Jerry, pain-racked and exhausted, back to his cell.

The questioning continued day after day—only the questions changed.

As months became years, the POWs learned the North Vietnamese game plan. "They wanted to break our will so we would do whatever they ordered," said Jerry. "Each step served a purpose. 1. Make us feel guilty. 2. Use threats. 3. Use punishment—torture. 4. Get the prisoner to apologize for wrongs against North Vietnam. 5. Do what they wanted—write a biography (personal information) or record a confession.

The North Vietnamese wanted propaganda. This meant information, pictures or anything to spread their ideas. They believed the United States, a larger country with more power and money, could defeat them on the battlefield. So they focused on turning the American people against the war. They mainly used television. But they also used journalists to write newspaper and magazine articles in their favor.

This is why their game plan's main goal was to get Prisoners of War to write about themselves or record a confession. They used it to show the world a prisoner had dishonored himself and his country.

Eagle and Owl repeatedly told Jerry he showed a bad attitude. He should cooperate and answer their questions. Next, Eagle used threats. He said if Jerry didn't cooperate, they couldn't promise his safety. They may turn him over to civilians to question him.

Civilians used severe punishment. If Jerry lost a leg or arm during the torture, they'd kill him. "I never knew what might happen next," said Jerry.

"One night, I was taken about midnight to be questioned—the third time that day. Owl and Eagle's excitement alerted me," said Jerry. "Owl waved a newspaper clipping in my face. It said Tschudy and I with Attack Squadron Seventy-five had been downed over North Vietnam.

"They knew I was flying an A6 Intruder. So, they tried to get me to admit it. I wouldn't say anything. Then they listed names of officers in my squadron. Evidently, they got them from another newspaper article."

Owl asked, "Is it not true, Denton, that Secretary of Defense McNamara watched your plane take off? Did he personally order you to bomb civilians?"

"They felt they now had a powerful weapon to hold over me," said Jerry. "I'd never met McNamara personally. But I'd never be able to convince them. This thought chilled my insides."

Codes

DRESSED ONLY IN HIS UNDERWEAR and drenched in sweat, Jerry writhed in pain on the bare concrete bunk. He didn't get a thin bamboo mat for several weeks. Infection had set in where the tendon came through the skin on his left thigh. Roaches and flies crawled everywhere including on him. His cell stank, because guards used the gutter outside the cell for a bathroom.

On the sixth day, Jerry took a bath. "An old guard took me to a covered but open-sided bath area. I had no shoes, so I walked barefoot through the filth. When I turned on the shower, only a few drops trickled out. The guard pointed toward a bucketful of water. Still wearing my underwear, I dumped the whole bucketful over my head. The startled guard laughed—his first and only time."

Jerry desperately wanted to talk to another prisoner. He heard a guard talking to someone down the hall. Later, Jerry risked calling to the person from his barred window. His voice echoed from the huge wall outside to the other prisoner. Air Force Major Larry Guarino answered him. After that, they talked a couple of times a day.

A daily schedule kept Jerry's mind active and helped resist despair. "I prayed, exercised, planned escape, and thought about family or friends," said Jerry. "I ate, napped, talked to Guarino and then repeated everything."

As the number of POWs increased, guards became strict. Prison officials didn't want POWs talking to each other, fearing that the prisoners might plan ways to resist.

So POWs communicated without talking. Most already knew Morse code, so they used it at first. It combined dots, dashes and spaces to stand for letters of the alphabet and numbers. Since they didn't have a telegraph to send the dots and dashes over wires, they used sound. A prisoner might tap on a wall once for a dot and thump with his fist for a dash. Or give a short whistle for a dot and a longer whistle for a dash. A cough or a scrape with a nail or broom also worked. Later, a simple tap code turned into the main form of sending messages. Teaching this code to new prisoners became a top priority.

Several years later, Jerry devised another code.

"Jerry Denton's famous 'Vocal Tap Code' was a favorite," said Jim Stockdale, another POW. "We emptied toilet buckets daily. Locked in the cell nearest the bucket dump, Jerry always emptied his last. Then he washed down the toilet platform. If Jerry wanted to send an urgent message, he'd signal everybody to distract the guard. This meant we spit, snorted and sneezed as we moved to and from the bucket dump. Then when Jerry washed down the area, he'd replace tap-code numbers. Numbers 1 or 2 became one cough or one snort, or two of either.... He'd send his urgent message," said Jim.

"Jerry often gave a five-minute speech while sweeping. He appeared to be serious about cleaning the area. But actually, he used vocal sounds as he 'swept' out a joke, a prayer, or important information.

"A prisoner coming back from a quiz, also used this code," said Jim. "He snorted and wheezed, giving us in solitary confinement a full report. The guard never suspected anything."

One day Jerry heard a voice from a cell say, "Go fishing!" The shower area had two drain holes. Left alone for a minute, Jerry searched one drain but found nothing. The next day, he discovered a matchstick lying across the other one. A note written on a scrap of paper with a burnt match hung down into the drain on a string. The message said: *If you read this, spit when you depart the latrine door.* Jerry spat and Lieutenant Commander Bob Shumaker knew he'd read the note. Jerry found scrap paper in the courtyard and later a piece of lead. From then on, he sometimes wrote messages—a risky way to communicate.

T-O-R-T-U-R-E

JERRY WAS THE HIGHEST-RANKING officer at New Guy Village, and he became camp commander there. More than once, he thought about Sister Mary Josephine's warning from eighth grade after he had led his whole class in skipping school. "It takes leadership to do what you've done. If you have that much influence over people you'd better be very careful how you use it!"

As a leader, he had to make hard choices. If he kept quiet and caused no trouble, he'd be okay. If he did what he felt right and honorable, he'd be punished.

As more planes were shot down, the prison became crowded. Officials moved some prisoners— including those causing trouble—to other Hanoi area prisons. In October, 1965, Jerry ended up in a prison nicknamed The Zoo, where guards stared through the door's peephole at a prisoner like he was an animal.

In April, 1966, Jerry refused to write a biography

or confession. Also accused of getting others to resist, he was taken back to the Hanoi Hilton.

A master torturer called Pigeye told Jerry he'd be tortured until he confessed his crimes.

Jerry often thought about Coach Overton, his high school football coach. He'd said, "To be a champion, you have to pay the price every minute, day in and day out." Jerry had done that, and he intended to continue! However, he didn't expect to survive, so he talked freely to Stockdale in a nearby cell. Jerry asked him to tell Jane that he loved her and wanted her to remarry.

"I felt no bitterness," Jerry said. "God had given me a full life."

The North Vietnamese tortured Jerry in a room nicknamed the Meathook Room. Pigeye handcuffed Jerry with his hands behind him. The guards kept him standing, and they beat him. He reeled around the cell and fell constantly. They yanked him up and beat him some more. Then they stopped and left him for a while with a bloody nose, cut lips, black eyes and bruised ribs.

When they returned, they got serious.

Jerry saw a small rope in Pigeye's hand. Jerry decided he was ready to lose an arm instead of his honor. He just wanted to get it over with.

Pigeye pulled Jerry's shirt sleeves down to protect his arms from scars. "Pigeye and another guard began roping one arm from shoulder to elbow. With each loop, one guard put his foot on my arm and pulled," said Jerry. "Then the other guard joined his strength to make it as tight as possible. When both arms were roped, they were tied together so closely that the elbows touched.

"The first pains came from the terrible pinching of the flesh. After about ten minutes, an agonizing pain began to flow through my arms and shoulders. My heart struggled to pump blood through the strangled veins. After about forty-five minutes, I went numb. As I fell backward, one finger on each hand spread out, and the weight of my body dislocated them."

A guard threw Jerry into a shower to revive. In a cell across the hall, a prisoner asked his name. When Jerry told him, he said, "God bless you, Jeremiah Denton. I'm Robbie Risner. You did a wonderful job at the Zoo."

Jerry replied that he wasn't doing one now.

Robbie said, "You are only human." These words coming from a tough, honorable officer (later a general) meant a lot.

The guard took Jerry from the shower to a quiz room. He mumbled something into a tape recorder.

Then, an officer held a pen in his hand and forced him to write. Jerry said later, "I was numb. Just numb."

However, Jerry had learned to "bounce back." He resisted until broken, recovered, and made them break him again. His mind had barely cleared before an officer told him he'd be interviewed on TV by the press. If he wasn't "polite" and didn't answer properly, he would be tortured more.

Jerry decided to find some way to use the press conference for his purposes.

On the night of the interview, Jerry entered a large room. Civilians, North Vietnamese officers, prison officials and journalists from several countries filled the room. A Japanese reporter interviewed Jerry. He tried to make Jerry smile. But, Jerry wanted to look haggard. Floodlights blinded him as he stared at the reporter. Jerry planned to give answers opposite to what the North Vietnamese wanted. But he acted polite and waited.

The reporter asked routine questions. Then he talked about the U.S. bombing North Vietnam.

Jerry gazed around as if in a daze. The blinding lights made him blink.

Suddenly, he had an idea.

He'd blink a message to the world! He looked directly into the camera and blinked in *Morse code!*

Blink eyes slowly once: **T;** then three more times, slowly: **O.**

In Morse code, he spelled:

T −

O − − −

R . − .

T −

U . . −

R . − .

E .

T O R T U R E.

While responding to the reporter's questions, Jerry blinked the desperate message over and over. The reporter's voice changed which got Jerry's attention. "Denton, what is your feeling toward your government's action?" asked the reporter.

Jerry licked his lips and thought carefully. "I don't know what is going on in the war now. My only sources are North Vietnamese radio, magazines, and newspaper. But whatever the position of my government, I agree with it. I support it. I will support it as long as I live!"

Jerry learned years later that Naval Intelligence got his Morse code message. It proved the North Vietnamese tortured POWs.

He thinks the North Vietnamese probably didn't learn about it until eight years later, in November, 1974. That is when he received the Navy Cross, not for blinking T-O-R-T-U-R-E, but for the brave answers that he gave the reporter about his government's actions.

This is the cover of a book written by Jerry about his experiences as a prisoner of war in North Vietnam. The photo shows Jerry blinking T-O-R-T-U-R-E during the television interview.

Freedom

THE HARDER THEIR CAPTORS tried to break some POWs, the more determined those POWs were not to give in.

The prisoners also inspired other prisoners to do the same.

The North Vietnamese kept the toughest POWs in solitary confinement. Still, the POWs were able to communicate. So in October, 1967, guards moved eleven "hard-core diehards" to a prison nicknamed Alcatraz.

The first fourteen months at Alcatraz were actually easier than life at the Hanoi Hilton. But then torture started back with a vengeance. Sometimes the torture was being kept in pitch-black cells. Sometime it was physical pain. Starvation diets. Little or no water to drink. And little or no sleep for days.

The torture continued for a year.

Arriving back at the Hanoi Hilton on December 9,

1969, the Alcatraz gang found things changing. In past wars, North Vietnamese had treated prisoners like human beings. Now, prison officials publicly admitted they had gone against this. However, they wanted to avoid punishment for their terrible behavior. Also, North Vietnam officials needed American aid (money to rebuild their country). If they released sick and half-starved prisoners, the U.S. wouldn't give it to them. So, they gave the prisoners more food and better health care.

On December 23, 1969, Jerry celebrated Jim Mulligan coming back as his roommate. For a few months in 1967, Jim and Jerry shared a cell. Other than that, Jerry had been in solitary confinement for over four years.

North Vietnam officials allowed POWs to have church services beginning in 1971.

The very first U.S. prisoner at Hanoi Hilton, Navy Lieutenant Everett Alvarez, Jr. had arrived in August 1964. He spent more than nine years in prison. During that time, the prison population gradually increased to nearly 350.

Richard Nixon was reelected president on November 8, 1972. He intended to keep his campaign promise to bring the POWs home.

Peace talks—which had been on and off since 1968—started again in Paris on January 8, 1973. On January 23, President Nixon announced the end of America's longest war.

In February, all POWs at the Hanoi Hilton came together. Jerry saw Bill Tschudy for the first time after more than seven years.

On February 12, 1973, the men marched out the Hanoi Hilton gate where they had entered. The sick and injured went first. Then, Everett Alvarez led the others in the order they were shot down.

Jerry, the thirteenth pilot shot down, went out as the senior officer of the first group. Buses took them to the Gia Lam airport. Each man walked up to a microphone and said his name. The North Vietnamese official repeated it. Then, the man walked toward the plane. On the other side of a long table, men and women in their blue U.S. Air Force uniforms were a welcome sight.

Seven years and seven months after he was shot down, Jerry was a free man again.

"Once we were in the air on the way to Clark Field in the Philippines, I was told that the senior officer was invited to make a statement upon arrival," said Jerry. "I thought about all the American fighting men who had given their lives.... I scratched out a few words and tried to memorize them. We covered the distance between captivity and freedom in one hour and forty-five minutes.

"There was a large crowd, and I felt shaky on the plane's steps. I saluted the flag and went to the microphone. I said, 'We are honored to have had the opportunity to serve our country under difficult circumstances. We are profoundly grateful to our Commander-in-Chief and to our nation for this day.' But I was strangely unfulfilled. I hadn't said quite all that

Jerry, just released from the North Vietnam prison, a free man and on his way home. He spoke on behalf of the first returning POWs at Clark Field in the Philippines.

was in my heart. Finally, unrehearsed words slipped from me: 'God bless America!' And I thought *Land that I love.*"

Homecoming

"ONE DAY MRS. DENTON was in my chair," said Jane's hairstylist, Judy Marshall. "The receptionist came and said I had an important phone call. It was from the Pentagon! My heart was beating so fast. We had been praying for Mrs. Denton and her family all these years. So we knew she was waiting for this call. She came to the phone with her hair in curlers. We all waited in silence.

"Mrs. Denton came back to my chair as calm as a cucumber. 'He's on the first plane,' she said. I hugged her and whispered we were all so pleased.

"I put her under the dryer and thought about the silent sacrifice she'd gone through raising her children. And her husband had sacrificed so much for our country.

"She surprised me and fell asleep under the dryer. When she woke up, she said, 'That was the best sleep I've had in seven years!'"

Jane and Jerry's welcome-home hug.

The Denton family along with thousands of others gathered at the Norfolk Naval Air Station. They came to greet Jeremiah Denton, now promoted to captain, and several other POWs returning home. The plane arrived just after midnight on February 15, 1973.

"I'll never forget the beautiful sight on TV of Mrs. Denton running toward him," said Judy Marshall. "And then their first embrace after all those years."

Jerry was overwhelmed when he saw his grown children plus meeting two daughters-in-law. His youngest child, Mary Beth, knew her father only from photographs. She was by then nine years old, and Madeleine and Michael were teenagers.

Jerry had many things on his mind when the family arrived at home. He asked them to spoil him and let him talk—and they did. They took an emotional rollercoaster ride from tears to laughter until daybreak. Jerry gave each child two precious gifts. First, he told a special memory of each one that he'd dwelled on in his cell. Second, he apologized and asked forgiveness for some little matter that he'd never allowed himself to forget. The children stored these gifts in their hearts.

"My mother was right," said Jerry. "She said we don't appreciate the simple things of life until we don't have them." He talked about food, sandals, clean clothes, water, soap and toilet tissue.

Jerry told them a story about praying for toilet tissue.

"Being punished for communicating, I had to kneel outside on concrete. I wore double-leg irons, and my hands were cuffed behind me. I knew the guard wouldn't give me any toilet tissue," he said. "So as I knelt in the sweltering heat with my head bowed, I prayed for a small favor.

"I threw my head back and peeped under my blindfold at the sky. A large leaf swirled and fluttered down toward me. Taking a sudden dive, it landed almost at my feet. The large leaf—9 inches by 6 inches—had a furry side. Perfect!" said Jerry.

"I twisted my body, and picked up the leaf with my cuffed hands. Then I tore it into four pieces. I worked my way to the nearby bucket, where I put the pieces to use. Another prayer answered."

He told of going back in his mind to his earliest memories. He thought of his mother and her faith. He remembered his outgoing father working in hotels. He recalled school friends and his roots in Mobile. This was a surprise to Jane, because she was always the one who wanted to visit relatives, not Jerry.

Jerry told them of God's presence and comfort in the worst of times—not only for him, but for many POWs. And he told them of his great love for our country and how he wanted to protect our freedom.

Senator Jeremiah A. Denton, Jr.

TWO MONTHS AFTER returning home from North Vietnam, Denton received a promotion to Rear Admiral. His last Navy assignment was in Norfolk, Virginia. He was Commandant of the Armed Forces Staff College for three and a half years.

Jerry wrote a book, *When Hell Was in Session*, assisted by Ed Brandt—a Norfolk newspaper editor. It was published in 1976.

NBC produced a television movie, *When Hell Was in Session*. Based on the book, it starred Hal Holbrook and Eva-Marie Saint.

By 1977, Jerry had retired from the Navy and returned to Mobile. He founded and led the non-profit organization "Coalition for Decency" and served as a consultant to the president of Spring Hill College in Mobile.

Jerry got a lot of attention after he returned from

North Vietnam. TV reporters and politicians often referred to his three sentence speech at Clark Field. Mobile held a huge parade in his honor. Then more publicity came with the publication of his book. The movie aired on national TV, and all of a sudden it seemed that everyone in American knew the name Jeremiah Denton.

Soon, important people asked Jerry to run for the United States Senate.

At first, Jerry turned them down. But important people didn't take *no* for an answer and kept asking Jerry to run. Finally, with the election just six months away, Jerry agreed.

Jerry believed that as a Senator he could help the country. He wanted to help make America a better place for husbands and wives to raise their children. He also wanted to make the United States a safer place to live.

Family and friends worked tirelessly, carrying his message all over Alabama. Jane and several of the children split up and went to different parts of the state. Day after day they appeared at club luncheons, county fairs and many other places. They talked about what Jerry would do if elected.

First, the Republicans had an election to see who would be their candidate for the Senate. After Jerry won, getting four out of every six votes, he had to run against the Democrat's candidate.

Ronald Reagan was running for president of the United States. The night before the election, Reagan made a speech on national television. He complimented Admiral Denton's "God Bless America" statement.

When the voting ended the next day, Jerry was Alabama's newest United States Senator.

He served from January 2, 1981 until January 2, 1987.

Ronald Reagan was elected president on the same day. In 1982, President Reagan gave a speech to the American people that was called the State of the Union address. "We don't have to turn to history books for heroes," Reagan said. "They are all around us. One who sits among you here tonight epitomized that heroism at the end of the longest imprisonment ever inflicted on men of our armed forces. Who can ever forget that night when we waited for television to bring us the scene of that first plane landing at Clark Field in the Philippines—bringing our POWs home. The plane door open and Jeremiah Denton came slowly down the ramp. He saluted our flag, thanked us for bringing them home, and said 'God bless America.'"

"The applause was tremendous," said Jim Denton. "Dad stood and thanked his fellow congressmen and the audience."

As a United States Senator, Denton was proud of

Senator Jeremiah Denton with President Ronald Reagan.

many accomplishments that included:

• Bringing jobs and income to Alabama from foreign trade.

• Helping convince other members of the Senate to provide tax money to complete the Tennessee-Tombigbee Waterway.

• Bringing Navy ships to Alabama when Mobile became a homeport.

• Recommending four judges whom the Senate confirmed as federal judges.

• Increasing national security.

• Writing laws and rules against terrorism.

• Serving in 1983 as an observer during an election in the Central American nation of El Salvador. Was key advisor to the President on efforts to replace the communist government with a free government.

• Serving on the Judiciary Committee and chairing the Sub-Committee on Security and Terrorism; Labor and Human Resources Committee and chairing the Sub-Committee on Aging, Family and Human Services; Armed Services Committee; and Veterans Affairs Committee.

Jerry also sponsored several government programs that he saw as important:

• Denton Adolescent Family Life Act provided education for teenagers about living a wholesome lifestyle, and helped both teenagers and their families when certain kinds of problems happened.

- The Denton Equal Access Act allowed students to meet voluntarily for fellowship, Bible reading, and prayer.

- The Denton Program allowed the U.S. military to transport charitable relief supplies world-wide on military aircraft whenever space was available at no expense to the private donor.

In 1983, Jerry formed the National Forum Foundation. Later, his son, James Denton, headed the research and education organization. It provided information and materials on issues involving national security, welfare reform and the family.

Epilogue

AS THE VIETNAM WAR neared its end, and the release of the POWs was near, a North Vietnamese officer asked Jerry what he would say when he got home. Jerry asked, "Why do you care what I say? There are hundreds of men who will speak when they get home."

"You are credible (honest), Denton," said the officer. "People will believe you."

"I'll tell them that through 1969 the North Vietnamese tortured us," he said. "You treated us worse than animals. But after that, you came off torture. To my knowledge, you no longer used extreme punishment."

"That is the truth," said the officer, "but others may not tell the truth."

"If there is any exaggeration, the senior officers will take care of it," Jerry replied.

Jerry's character was formed in his family. The faith of his mother and the influence of his father helped shape it. He had learned Bible stories and verses that he recalled from memory when there were no Bibles in prison. He prayed. And he sang songs to himself and to other prisoners. He knew the guards would probably beat him, but he did it anyway.

"The strength and goodness of Jerry Denton's character are best known to us who were in prison with him. We saw and felt his power at times when the going was the very toughest. He shunned the relative safety of a *low profile*. He withstood the sure pain and isolation of leadership," said fellow POW Captain Eugene "Red" McDaniel.

After Jerry retired from the Navy, he founded a number of organizations to help make the United States a more wholesome nation. Jerry worked to show American citizens the importance of high morals, of a strong religious faith, of helping poor people and others who were in need. He worked to let others know the importance of living in a free country, and that living in a free country meant that every citizen should work to keep it strong and free.

Hurricane Katrina badly damaged the Denton's home on Fowl River in Theodore, Alabama. Jane, Jerry and their son, Bill, moved to Williamsburg, Virginia in 2007. They wanted to be closer to other Denton children. A few months later, Jane had a heart attack. She died on Thanksgiving Day at age 81. They have seven children, fourteen grandchildren and three great-grandchildren.

Jerry, in his late eighties at the time of this writing, continues to provide leadership for the Admiral Jeremiah Denton Foundation. He is on many boards, including the Thomas Moore Law Center.

Jerry's experience of blinking TORTURE is featured in an exhibit called "Eyewitness, American Originals from the National Archives, Gripping Eyewitness Accounts of Moments in U.S. History." He is one of twenty-five Americans throughout U.S. history chosen to be in this exhibit.

Jeremiah A. Denton, Jr.

Rear Admiral Jeremiah A. Denton

Major Military Decorations:

Navy Cross

Department of Defense Distinguished Service Medal

Navy Distinguished Service Medal

Three Silver Stars

Distinguished Flying Cross

Five Bronze Stars

Two Air Medals

Two Purple Hearts

Combat Action Ribbon

Anne Chancey Dalton

Rear Admiral
Jeremiah A. Denton, Jr.

1924 Born July 15, in Mobile, Alabama to Irene Steele Denton and Jeremiah A. Denton, Sr.

1926-30 Lived in hotels in El Paso, Texas.

1931-32 Moved back to Mobile where the Denton family lived in a house for the first time.

1932-35 Lived in Chicago.

1936 Moved back to Mobile with his mother and brothers and lived in the Bienville Hotel with grandparents. His father moved to Houston, Texas to work.

1938 Irene and Jeremiah Denton, Sr. divorced. Irene bought a house in Mobile.

1942 Graduated from Mobile's McGill Institute.

1942-43 Attended Springhill College in Mobile.

1943-46 Attended United States Naval Academy. Graduated with honors June 5, 1946.

Jeremiah A. Denton, Jr.: Vietnam War Hero

As a Naval Academy Midshipman.

1946 Married Jane Maury June 6, 1946 in the Naval Academy Chapel.

Began career in United States Navy.

1957-58 "Haystack Concept" developed by Denton while he was Fleet Air Defense Officer with the Sixth Fleet in the Mediterranean. His ideas pioneered new developments in anti-submarine warfare, attack aviation, and air defense. Gained him two nominations for the Stephen Decatur Award, honoring the year's most outstanding naval operational achievement.

1958 Attended and graduated from the Armed Services Staff College.

1963-64 Attended Naval War College. His master's thesis earned him degrees from the War College and George Washington University. His thesis on international affairs received top honors by earning the prestigious President's Award. In 1964, he received a Master of Arts in International Affairs degree from George Washington University.

1965 July 18, plane shot down in North Vietnam.

1965-73 Prisoner of war in North Vietnam.

1973 February 12 Spokesperson for the first group of POWs returning to the United States.

February 15, after midnight, arrived with other POWs at Norfolk Naval Air Station. Reunited with family after seven years and seven months.

April Promoted to Rear Admiral.

April 27 City of Mobile designated Jerry Denton Day and had parade in his honor.

1973-77 Served as Commandant of the Armed Forces Staff College in Norfolk, Va.

1976 Publication by Readers Digest Press: *When Hell Was In Session* by Rear Admiral Denton with Ed Brandt.

1977 Retired from Navy. Returned to Mobile. Founded and led the non-profit organization Coalition for Decency. Consultant to the president of Spring Hill College.

1979 NBC television movie, *When Hell Was In Session*, released. Won the Dean Rusk-sponsored Peabody Award from the University of Georgia in 1979.

1980 Elected U.S. Senator from Alabama in November.

1981-87 U.S. Senator from Alabama.

1981 Became a Knight of the Sovereign Military Order of Malta, a distinguished Catholic religious order dedicated to serving the sick and poor and defending the faith.

1983 Observer of the El Salvadoran election plus key advisor to President on stopping aggression in Central America. Founded the National Forum Foundation—a research and educational organization that provided information and materials on issues involving national security, welfare reform and the family.

1985 Sponsored legislation creating the Denton Program, an international aid program working on a space-available basis with the U.S. military to transport critical supplies and equipment to people in need.

1986 Lost U.S. Senate election by less than one percent of votes.

2005 Hurricane Katrina badly damaged Denton home in Theodore, Alabama.

2007 Jane, Jerry and Bill Denton moved to Williamsburg, Virginia.

Thanksgiving Day, Jane died of complications from a heart attack several weeks earlier.

2011 The Denton Program still allows the U.S. military to transport charitable relief supplies world-wide on military aircraft whenever space is available at no expense to the private donor. In December, firefighting equipment and six fire trucks were shipped to an area in great need.

Admiral Denton continues to speak out on issues involving the United States. He also still enjoys playing golf.

About the Author

Anne Chancey Dalton likes acting, adventure, history and mystery. A classroom teacher for twenty-six years, she is now a teaching artist specializing in theatre and creative writing. She authored two historical mysteries: *Massacre Island* (original name of Dauphin Island) about the French settling Alabama; and *Dream Ghost* set in the 1850s in Cahaba, Alabama.

She portrays characters from her books, biblical and historical characters in dramatic monologues.

Anne and Perry have two children by birth, nine other children, and many, many grand and great-grandchildren.